PRAISE FOR

CAGED WISDOM

"*Caged Wisdom: Learning to See through the Bars* captures the words of wisdom from the Living Bible for easy reading. It outlines the basic secrets for a successful and fulfilling life if the principals are followed consistently. This book will make a great study guide for offenders or ex-offenders in or out of prison. It will provide hope and inspiration to all who read it. It has enhanced my life, and I find myself picking up the book daily for guidance and inspiration. It is my distinct feeling that you won't regret having this book throughout your journey in life."

—Bobby Battle, former Oklahoma
State Penitentiary inmate

"*Caged Wisdom: Learning to See through the Bars* is a great tool for conveying the wisdom and hope found in Scripture. It is often difficult for those who are unfamiliar with the Bible or paralyzed with feeling hopeless to get what they need just by picking up a Bible to read. *Caged Wisdom: Learning to See through the Bars* brings out nuggets of truth from the gold mine of God's Word, making it easily accessible for everyone. I highly recommend *Caged Wisdom: Learning to See through the Bars* for those incarcerated or for anyone needing the encouragement and wisdom that only God can provide."

—Leo E. Brown,
Agency Chaplain and Volunteer Coordinator
Oklahoma Department of Corrections
Member and Past Regional Manager,
American Correctional Chaplains Association

CAGED WISDOM

CAGED WISDOM

LEARNING TO SEE THROUGH THE BARS

DAN M. REYNOLDS

TATE PUBLISHING
AND ENTERPRISES, LLC

Published by Tate Publishing & Enterprises, LLC
127 E. Trade Center Terrace | Mustang, Oklahoma 73064 USA
1.888.361.9473 | www.tatepublishing.com

Tate Publishing is committed to excellence in the publishing industry. The company reflects the philosophy established by the founders, based on Psalm 68:11,
"The Lord gave the word and great was the company of those who published it."

Book design copyright © 2012 by Tate Publishing, LLC. All rights reserved.
Cover design by Kenna Davis
Interior design by Chelsea Womble

Published in the United States of America

ISBN: 978-1-61777-984-8
1. Religion / Biblical Studies / Wisdom Literature
2. Self-Help / Spiritual
12.11.22

DEDICATION

This book is dedicated to all those incarcerated in prisons or jails. This book will help all those who want to know what God really wants us to know and how he wants us to live our lives.

Don't forget those in jail. (Hebrews 13:3).

TABLE OF
CONTENTS

INTRODUCTION

As I have read the Bible, I always thought that it contained the secrets to life. The Bible gives us words of wisdom to live by, and by following them, one will be successful. Many will not pick up the Bible and read it from cover to cover. They have a tendency to get lost in it. I have selected and extracted specific scriptures that I believe God wants us to know. The book shows us how to live a successful life using God's direction and guidance. This book shows us how God wants us to live and cohabitate with one another. The format is for easy reading and studying. The scriptures have been paraphrased, and each chapter contains a summary. Not each chapter in the Bible is represented.

As I read the Bible, I highlighted verses that gave instruction regarding how one should live their life. I wanted my children to read and know the secrets of a successful life. As I finished typing the highlighted areas, I realized these principles would also apply and benefit inmates. They could take advantage of the time they have and learn what they must do to live a productive and fruitful life once released and returned to society. Applying these principles will aid in their success and hopefully prevent them from returning to prison.

In addition, this book will also help those who need a significant change in their lives. The way they are living is not working, and they may be looking for another avenue. This book tells us how we should live our life according to God.

One will find the peace and joy God wants them to have if they adopt and follow the words of wisdom.

EXODUS

1. God does not want you to worship any other God than him (20:3).

2. God is a possessive God, and you are forbidden to worship any image, statue, animal, etc., other than God (20:5).

3. God does not want you to use His name in a disrespectful manner (20:7).

4. The seventh day is a holy day, which is called the Sabbath. Many refer to Sunday as their Sabbath day, the day of worship and rest. On this day, you are not to do any work of any kind, nor shall your sons and daughters (20:8).

5. You are to honor your father and mother (20:12).

6. Do not commit murder (20:13).

7. Do not commit adultery (20:14).

8. Do not steal (20:15).

9. Do not lie (20:16).

10. Do not want or desire your neighbor's possessions or anything else he may have (20:17).

In Exodus, very early in the Bible, God speaks specifically about what you need to do or not do to have a good life. He speaks of crimes you are not to commit. He conveys the message that you are not to worship anyone but him. He does not want you to worship idols in this world. He wants you to focus on him. He wants you to show respect to his name and not use it in vain. God lists the commandments he gave to Moses for us to live by in this world. He wants us to honor and respect our parents and not murder, cheat on our spouses, steal, or lie. He does not want us to envy what others have, but to be content with what we have. We would have a lot less inmates if the basic commandments of God were not violated.

A good start to a good life is to obey God's wishes and see what happens. Trust him and give him a chance to work in your life, but you must work and practice his ways. Has your way worked for you? We have all sinned and have fallen short of his expectations. It may not always be easy, but you have to continually try to get better each day—to be a better person. Stay in his Word and learn what he has to say. Many of those that violate His commandments end up in prisons and jails. It is never too late to begin a personal transformation; the choice is yours. Ask for his forgiveness and intervention. Ask him what he wants for your life and that *His* will be done.

DEUTERONOMY

1. God is a jealous God; therefore, you are not to worship any living or non-living thing other than God (5:8-10).

2. You are not to use God's name to make a promise you do not plan to keep (5:11).

3. You are not to do any kind of work on the Sabbath (5:12).

4. God wants you to love him with all your heart, soul, and might (6:5).

5. The ultimate life comes by obeying God's every command (8:3).

6. God will punish you to provide guidance and direction (8:5).

7. Tithing is giving ten percent of our earnings to God. God's purpose and teaching of tithing is to ensure you put God first in your lives (14:23).

8. You are not to convict anyone based solely on one witness (19:15).

9. You are not to show mercy to a false witness (19:21).

10. If you disobey God's laws, he will send plagues upon you and your children (28:58-59).

11. You are to obey all God's commandments (30:2).

12. By obeying God's laws, he will cleanse your hearts and the hearts of your children and of your children's children, and turn his curses on your enemies (30:6-8).

13. Make the decision to love and obey God, he is your life throughout your time on earth (30:20).

In Deuteronomy, God says he is a jealous God and he does not want us to worship anyone or anything else in this world. He demands respect from you, and blessings will be bestowed upon you if you do what he wants you to do in this world. He wants your love, and he will punish you and your children to help direct you on the right path in life. You must rest on the Sabbath as he did when he created the earth. It is a holy day of rest. God wants you to trust him. He is on your side and watching out for your best interests. If you obey God's commandments, he will begin to cleanse your heart and the hearts of your children. God also says that if you obey his commandments, he will take his curses and turn them against your enemies.

JOSHUA

1. Obey all God's commandments; in doing so, you will be successful in everything you do (22:4-5).

2. God has a plan for your life. Love God and seek and follow his plan he has for you (22:5).

In Joshua, God says all you have to do to be successful in all your endeavors is to obey and follow his commands. He has a plan for you; you just have to seek and find it and do what he wishes and watch everything fall into place for you. God begs for your obedience and for you to begin doing right so he can unveil his blessings he has in store for you. It may be easier than what you think!

1 SAMUEL

1. God sees a man's inner thoughts and intentions, whereas man judges by the exterior appearance (16:7).

First Samuel says that God knows what you are thinking and what your intentions are at all times. Man may only see the exterior appearance and does not always know your intentions or your thought processes. Don't try to fool God, because he knows you better than you know yourself; he is the one who created you. Partner with God to help you in this world; don't turn your back to him. He is there to help you, not to hurt you. Trust him.

1 KINGS

1. Seek God's will and strive to do what he wants you to do (8:58).

In 1 Kings, God wants us near him, to obey him and honor him. He desires a relationship with you. If you don't know what God's will is for you, ask him in prayer. Aggressively seek to find what he wants you to do in this world. Simply obey him and find his will for you. You will then find the peace and joy he wants you to have. Again, he wants you to trust him.

JOB

1. Seek wisdom from wise men; don't make the same mistakes they have made. Those who have no hope have not discovered God (8:10-13).

2. Going through life without God results in endless struggles, barriers, obstacles, failures, and frustration. How much turmoil and agony can one take? (8:14).

3. By aligning up to God's will, you will be filled with laughter and joy (8:21).

4. Get rid of your sins and leave them behind, then stretch out your hands to him. You will have courage and confidence because you have hope, but more importantly, you have discovered God (11:13-14, 18).

5. God is a good God and a gracious God. He is not filled with wickedness and unfairness (34:12). God and his Spirit appear to us in many

forms. For example, lightning bolts directed by his hands make us stop in our tracks. Thunder makes us listen and pay attention to the heavens above. He sends us storms, sometimes as punishment and other times to encourage us with his loving kindness (37:12-13).Take heed to what he is conveying to us. May we listen to him on our own accords and our free will?

The Book of Job is a book of faith, inspiration, suffering, and hope. It shows the powers of God and what God may allow in our lives. We may not understand it, but there is a purpose for what he does and what he allows us to go through in this world. He is a just and fair God. We are ultimately rewarded for our faith and obedience to him.

PSALMS

1. Salvation is from God, which brings us joy (3:8).

2. To avoid judgment, we are to confess our sins to God as soon as we are aware of them (32:6).

3. God watches closely those that are doing good (34:15).

4. God wants us to have strict control of what we say, how we say it, and when we say it. The tongue can do serious harm in our lives as well as other's. God wants us to work hard to make peace with all (34:13-14).

5. God will hear the good man when he cries for help and will come to his rescue (34:17).

6. God is sensitive to those who are humble and who are sincerely sorry for their sins. These individuals go through life experiencing problems as well, but they have God's assistance, direction, and wisdom. God may even inter-

vene and prevent accidents from occurring (34:18-20).

7. God wants you to be patient, and He will act in his own time. Be persistent in doing well, and your blessings will follow in due time. If you have doubt, pray for a renewed hope. If your heart is in turmoil, ask for his quiet calm to come upon you. Be delighted in the Lord (94:19).

8. God wants you to honor him and do so with joy and without reservation (100:4).

9. God gave us children as a gift from him. Children are his reward to us (127:3). What a tremendous gift! What joy and happiness they bring us.

10. God has a plan for your life, and he has constructively planned each day out for you, even before you took your first breath. Every day has been recorded in your book! (139:16).

11. Ask God to search our minds and souls and test our thoughts. Ask God to make you a better Christian today than what you were yesterday. Strive to find closeness with God (139:23).

In Psalms, God reveals that salvation comes from him and him alone. God wants us to confess our sins when we first become aware of them so we can avoid his judgment. Sincerely be sorry for your sins and ask for his forgiveness. If we want a good, long life, we must control our tongues—what we say and how we say it. Spend your time doing good and try hard to have peace with all on earth. God loves the good man who has good thoughts and intentions. He does not want these people to hurt or to be harmed. He will protect those from harm and even accidents. Be humble and be delighted in the Lord with true joy in your hearts. Give thanks to God for all he provides to you. Children are a true gift from God, and how your life changes as a new parent. You see the world a lot differently after the birth of a child. What compassion, understanding, and joy one feels! How your heart tugs at you for the sight of trials, struggles, and turmoil of others. As I reflect on the birth of my son and the love and joy I felt, I think about what a sacrifice God made when he sent his son, Jesus, to suffer and die on the cross, so we can share eternal life with him and have our sins forgiven. What love was expressed with such a sacrifice of his own son? I really didn't understand that love until my son was born. How much love would I have to have to sacrifice my son for others to live?

What a blessing to find that peace God wants you to have. God has a personal plan for you. It is recorded in a book. Every day has been planned. How will your life end?

PROVERBS

...King Solomon of Israel, David's son; he wrote these to teach his people how to live—he wanted to make the simple-minded wise (1:2-4).

1. According to God, for a man to find wisdom, he must trust and obey God (1:7-9).

2. God wants you to listen and be attentive to your parents (1:9).

3. If you choose to disobey or turn from God, you will experience the full terrors of the pathway you have chosen. Choose God, and you will have joy, peace, comfort, and protection, as well as wisdom and common sense (1:29-32; 2:1).

4. Put God first in your life; be kind and truthful, and you will find success and favor with God and man. One who listens and obeys God will find wisdom and good sense (2:1).

5. God requests that you give him ten percent of your earnings as you practice making him first in your life. In doing so, he will bless you with much more than you give. Trust him and watch the results (3:9-10).

6. Anyone willing to be corrected is on the pathway to life. God tells us to have two goals in life to strive for: wisdom and common sense. Wisdom is to know and do the right things in life. Having wisdom and common sense will keep us from defeat, disaster, and going off the righteous pathway of life. God wants us to seek correction in our lives if we need to be corrected. If we refuse correction or criticism, we will find poverty and disgrace (3:21; 10:17).

7. God does not want us to talk so much. Communicate with restraint (10:19).

8. Having God's blessing is our greatest wealth (10:22).

9. The employer's greatest pain is a lazy employee (10:26).

10. Good people will always have God's blessing (10:30).

11. God will protect good men in all situations, but will ignore evil men (11:8).

12. Speaking evil words hurts and is non-productive (11:9).

13. Those who are good maintain God's blessing forever. God will rescue and bless the good (11:21).

14. God will bless the good man and punish the wicked (12:2).

15. Those who are wicked will never find success (12:3).

16. You will find a good man with honest thoughts; a wicked man plots evil (12:5).

17. A wicked man is full of lies, but a good man's best defense is his honesty (12:13).

18. When insulted by others, stay calm and restrained (12:16).

19. The results of practicing honesty will outlast those of telling lies. Lies will soon surface and be known to all (12:19).

20. God wants you to work hard and become a leader. Those who are lazy will never know success (12:24).

21. Control your tongue and avoid problems. (13:3).

22. Being good throughout your life will reap sweet benefits (13:6).

23. Those who have money without God are poor. Those who have no money but know God are rich (13:7).

24. A light shines in a good man, whereas the wicked lives alone and in darkness (13:9).

25. Be humble and seek wise counsel (13:10). Determination is the first step to becoming wise.

26. Those in poverty and disgrace have refused criticism. Those who listen to criticism find themselves on the road to righteousness (13:18).

27. Associate with wise men and become wise. Associate with the wicked and become wicked (13:20).

28. Discipline your son; this is a sign of love, care, and concern for his well-being (13:24).

29. Doing right pleases God (14:2).

30. Keep your temper under control so you are not vulnerable in making grave mistakes (14:17).

31. To hate or scorn the poor is a sin in God's eyes (14:21).

32. God will grant mercy and quietness for those who are good (14:22).

33. Talk tends to result in poverty, where work tends to produce profit (14:23).

34. Control your anger so you won't make mistakes you will regret (14:29).

35. Being positive and having a good outward disposition and attitude is said to lengthen ones longevity (14:30).

36. When you help the poor, it pleases and honors God (14:31).

37. God is always watching the good as well as the wicked (15:3).

38. Success is seen when you commit your work to God (16:3).

39. It is better to be poor and humble than have a proud spirit and wealth (16:19).

40. Don't be idle and inactive, because you may be vulnerable to evil temptations (16:27).

41. Those who find God have purified hearts (17:3).

42. Do not mock the poor (17:5).

43. Do not be joyous in other's misfortunes (17:5).

44. The grandfather's crowning glory is his grandchildren (17:6).

45. Badgering about mistakes will part the best of friends (17:9).

46. Do not be rebellious (17:11).

47. Don't fall in the trap of getting into disagreements and fights with others (17:14).

48. Is it wise to pay a rebel's tuition who has no interest in finding the truth? (17:16).

49. Having a cheerful heart is good for the soul and lasting health (17:22).

50. A child is a gift from God, but one who is rebellious brings grief to his father and a disappointment to his mother (17:25).

51. Nothing is good about sin; it brings disgrace to all associated with it (18:3).

52. A foolish man is always fighting and arguing. His words hurt him (18:6-7).

53. A wise man is open and seeks new ideas (18:15).

54. Don't talk to the extreme or excessively. Too much talk may result in negative results (18:21).

55. Finding a good wife is a blessing from God and keeps a man from sinning (18:22).

56. It is always better to be a poor man and honest than a rich man and dishonest (19:1).

57. Seeking wisdom will result in your success (19:8).

58. A liar will always surface to the top for all to see (19:9).

59. Overlook insults and suppress anger (19:11).

60. Follow God's commandments and do not violate them. Violations of his commandments may result in death (19:16).

61. God will repay you graciously if you help to meet the needs of the poor (19:17).

62. Disciplining your son will ensure his hope and potential success in the future (19:18).

63. Helping a short-tempered man is futile (19:19).

64. Study to be wise and seek wisdom all you can so you can make good decisions that are pleasing to God (19:20).

65. Practicing kindness makes you attractive (19:22).

66. It is displeasing to God to mistreat or disrespect your parents (19:26).

67. Do not listen to those who teach the things you know are wrong (19:27).

68. Don't take in hard liquor; it results in negative and destructive behaviors (20:1).

69. God will honor a man who can stay out of a fight. Only fools want to fight (20:3).

70. You may have to plow in the cold to reap the harvest (20:4).

71. It is a great birthright to have an honest father (20:7).

72. The actions of a child can display his character; what he does in life will be pure and right (20:11).

73. Bless God every day for your eyesight, hearing, your arms and legs, fingers and toes, and to be able to get up out of bed in the morning. Not everyone can say that. Be thankful for what you have rather than what you don't have (20:12).

74. Stay awake and alert and work hard, and you will have plenty of food (20:13).

75. It is better to have good sense than expensive jewels (20:15).

76. God will punish a man who curses his father or mother (20:20).

77. Don't inflict evil methods on others who are evil to you. Let God handle it (20:22).

78. Inflicting severe punishment on those who commit crimes is a sign of a wise leader (20:26).

79. A secure leader is one who is kind, honest, and fair to all (20:28).

80. The young man's glory is seen in his strength, and with an old man, it is seen through his years of experience (20:29).

81. Evil can be chased out of one's heart if the punishment hurts enough (20:30).

82. If gain is sought dishonestly and is short-lived, is it worth the risk in the first place? (21:6).

83. Some say it is better to live in an attic than to stay with a crabby woman in a nice comfortable home (21:9).

84. Don't ignore the cries of the poor if you don't want God to ignore you in your time of crisis (21:13).

85. The righteous will always prevail, and the wicked will always fall short (21:18).

86. Attempting to do good deeds by displaying love and kindness to our neighbor will honor God, and it will be viewed as an act of righteousness (21:21).

87. Keeping your mouth closed reduces the likelihood you will get in trouble (21:23).

88. A godly man will consider and listen to all options, whereas an evil man is steadfast and stubborn (21:29).

89. A wise man sees trouble ahead and develops a plan to resolve it, whereas the unwise man plunders forward and suffers the consequences (22:3).

90. Respecting God will lead a man to success, honor, and a long life (22:4).

91. The rebel prepares a dangerous path for himself (22:5).

92. Teach the young and show them the right path to take in life and he will stay on it. If he veers off at times, he will eventually return to it (22:6).

93. A man who feeds the poor will find happiness in his life (22:9).

94. Isolate a mocker, and you will eliminate any tension, conflict, and arguing (22:10).

95. God will protect the good and destroy the wicked (22:12).

96. Don't be lazy (22:13).

97. Stay away from prostitutes and sexual sin. Those in sexual sin are cursed by God and are entangled in it. Run from sexual sin (22:14).

98. Punishment is a good remedy for a rebellious fellow (22:15).

99. It is not wise to take advantage of the poor (22:22-23).

100. Teach others of lessons learned that caused you to be wise (22:17-19).

101. Don't steal from the poor or from the sick or unfortunate (22:22).

102. Stay away from angry people and those who are short-tempered; it could be harmful to you (22:24-25).

103. Don't countersign a loan because it puts you at unnecessary risks (22:26).

104. Don't work at getting rich (23:4).

105. Don't associate with those you consider to be evil or have evil ways (23:6).

106. Accept and welcome criticism; strive to improve yourself (23:12).

107. Don't fail to discipline your children when needed. This may rescue them from hell (22:13-14).

108. As long as you attempt to do the right thing for the right reason and you repent for your sins and ask God for forgiveness, there is hope (22:17-18).

109. Don't associate with those who get drunk or are considered to be radicals. They will pull you in and drag you down with them (23:19-21).

110. Listen to the wisdom of your father and do not discount your mother's life experiences (23:22).

111. Don't let the things in life that shine entice you into deception and sin (23:31).

112. Don't be jealous of those not of God; stay clear of the ungodly (24:1).

113. A man of wisdom is stronger than a weight lifter (24:5).

114. Wisdom is more powerful than brute strength (24:5).

115. You are not a good example if you break at the first taste of failure (24:10).

116. If you know a man who is innocent, don't stand back and let him be executed (24:11-12).

117. There is hope for you once you decide to become wise (24:13-14).

118. The evil man's days are numbered, and he will be dealt with accordingly (24:19-20).

119. Establish a strong and sturdy foundation before building upon it (24:27).

120. Accept criticism gladly and be honored by others (25:12).

121. Be a faithful and loyal employee to those who have invested and trusted you to provide a service to them. Don't turn on those who provided opportunities to you. Do you bite the hand that feeds you? (25:13).

122. Soft tongues can demolish and destroy hard bones (25:15).

123. Don't over-visit your friends and neighbors (24:17).

124. Don't gossip to your friends about others (25:18).

125. Don't think you deserve more than what you get. Be content with what you have (25:27).

126. Don't fall in the trap of acting out like a rebel. You will act foolish like he does (26:4-5).

127. Don't recognize or give credence to a rebel (26:8).

128. Don't be conceited (26:12).

129. Gossip creates unnecessary tension (26:20).

130. Don't brag or boast to others about your accomplishments or future plans (27:1).

131. Don't show or give praise to yourself (27:2).

132. Don't show or express jealous tendencies (27:4).

133. Don't turn your back on a friend (27:10).

134. A sensible son honors his father (27:11).

135. You can tell a lot about a man by the friends he keeps (27:19).

136. It is wise to always know where you stand and the status of your business interests (27:24).

137. Men of God are courageous and confident (28:1).

138. Stability is a sign of honest sensible leaders (28:2).

139. You have to fight evil to maintain justice (28:4).

140. Godly people understand the importance of maintaining law and order (28:5).

141. Wise men obey the laws; those who disregard the laws are a shame to their families (28:7).

142. Prayers from those who violate the law fall on deaf ears (28:9).

143. If you make a mistake, admit it, and you will get a second chance. Success does not come when you fail to see your mistakes (28:13).

144. God will bless those who serve and obey him. He will not rescue the unbelievers who don't care (28:18).

145. Hard work will bring honor and prosperity (28:19).

146. A rich reward awaits a man who does the right thing (28:20).

147. Don't try to get rich quickly and lose focus on the real purposes of life (28:22).

148. A man who steals from his parents is no better than one who commits murder (28:24).

149. Avoid being greedy with the things of the world (28:25).

150. When you give to the poor, God will provide for all your needs (28:27).

151. The wicked are not friends to the poor (28:27).

152. Don't start fights (29:8).

153. Don't argue with others (29:9).

154. Pray for your enemies (29:10).

155. A leader will retain his position when he shows fairness to the poor (29:14).

156. Paddling a child will instill long-term lessons not likely to be forgotten (29:15).

157. Godly leaders will outlast those who are evil. Evil leaders tend to have evil followers (29:16).

158. Providing constructive discipline to a child will result in a state of peace and contentment (29:17).

159. A fool has more of a chance than a quick-tempered man (29:20).

160. Don't be prideful (29:23).

161. One shows self-hatred if he assists a criminal, for he knows better but participates anyway (29:24).

162. There is no need to fear man; trusting in God will ensure your safety and protection (29:25).

163. Don't mock your parents (30:17).

The book of Proverbs contains the true lessons of life. Proverbs displays the true wisdom of God. It reminds us to respect and honor our parents. Proverbs tells us to be wise and seek God's purpose and plan. Be truthful and kind. Take care of the poor and the less fortunate. Seek wisdom and common sense. Watch your tongue, for what you say can get you in deep trouble. Work hard and don't be lazy. Give your first ten percent of your wages to God to ensure you put him first in your life. Don't lose your temper, and stay calm and trust in the Lord to take care of your battles. Commit your work to the Lord. It is better to have faith and be poor than to be rich and not know God. It is a good thing to discipline your child; this teaches valuable lessons on down the road. Stay away from hard liquor and drunkards and those who are ungodly. Run from sexual sin and don't fall in that trap that is difficult to free yourself from. Enjoy seeking God's plan for you as you become wiser. Don't be a braggart or one that is conceited. Be kind, honest, trustworthy, a seeker of wisdom; take care of the poor and always do right! God will not listen to those who continue to violate the law. Proverbs contains the do's and don'ts of human behavior.

ECCLESIASTES

1. Follow through on your commitments and promises to God. You are better off not making commitments and promises that you cannot keep (5:4-5).

2. Finding the right job or niche in life is a true gift from God (5:19-20).

3. Your life was planned out before your birth, so why argue about what life has in store for you? (6:10).

4. The more you talk, the more people get lost in your message (6:11).

5. Sadness is better than happiness, because sadness has a profound effect on us that may have positive outcomes (7:3).

6. Expect God's blessing if you are aggressive enough to take on every assigned task (7:18).

7. Some may believe that sinning may go without punishment because the punishment is not sudden. Don't be fooled by such reasoning (8:11).

8. Ones that have no hope have no ambition to do good because the end result will be death (9:2-3).

9. God has given you a wife as the best reward for your earthly deeds (9:9).

10. It is the entire duty of men to fear God and obey his commandments. God will be the ultimate judge of all we do, both good and bad. This includes those things we do in private, as well as what we do in public (12:13).

In Ecclesiastes, God wants us to keep our promises to him and to not make promises we cannot or will not keep. Accept your niche in life and be joyful that you have found it. People should not fret over their destiny, because it has already been planned out before birth. A wife is God's best reward for those living on earth. God conveys his final conclusion, and that is to fear him and obey his commandments. Have you ever asked yourself why you are in the position you are in now? Is God trying to tell you something? Is he trying to get your attention to turn around your evil ways and continued behavior?

ISAIAH

1. You know right from wrong; listen to God and don't pay attention to the gossip of others (51:7).

2. Feed those who are hungry, and God will keep you healthy and provide the proper guidance and direction in your life (58:10).

3. Honor the Sabbath with a delightful spirit (58:13).

4. Sin will eventually cut you off from God, and he will no longer listen to your cries (59:2).

5. If you don't find God's blessing, search deep within yourself and find any sin or evilness stored within you preventing you from receiving God's blessing (59:9).

The book of Isaiah wants us to listen to God and to discard one's gossip and scorn. He reminds us to keep the Sabbath a holy day and to not work. He also reminds us to take care of the poor by feeding them and help those in trouble; you will be blessed by doing so. If sin continues to be a part of your life, God will no longer listen or protect you. Obey and trust God so blessings can be bestowed upon you.

LAMENTATIONS

1. If one strikes you on your cheek, turn and let him strike you on the other cheek. God may allow grief, but he will also display compassion. He does not like afflicting sorrow on us (3:30).

2. Why do we complain when God punishes us for our sins? Rather we should repent and ask for forgiveness and get on the right path and on the right side of God. Is it so hard to trust, obey and have faith in God? (3:39).

In the book of Lamentations, God tells us to turn the other cheek to those who strike us, for the Lord will not abandon us forever. God allows grief to come into our lives, but he also provides compassion. Rather than complaining for our misfortunes, we need not complain but repent for our sins and ask God to forgive us.

NAHUM

1. God is a jealous God and he takes vengeance on those who hurt his people (1:2).

2. Cyclones, tornadoes and severe storms are a display of God's power in heaven (1:3).

In the book of Nahum, God tells us that he is a jealous God and will go after those who hurt his people. He will destroy those who hurt his people. Don't always try to fight all your battles; turn it over to God and let him handle it his way. He shows his great power through natural events such as cyclones, tornadoes, and storms.

ZEPHANIAH

1. Always be a humble servant and do the right thing for the right reason (2:3).

In Zephaniah, the message is direct and to the point. God wants us to be humble and to just do right! God does not want us to draw attention to ourselves, become proud, or expect praise and attention. Have a humble spirit!

MATTHEW

1. Be obedient to every word of God is what we need to do today (4:4).

2. A humble man is a fortunate man who will be comforted in times of mourning (5:3-4).

3. You will be in danger of judgment if you are angry in your own home (5:22).

4. You will be held accountable, so don't say harmful words or curse at others (5:22).

5. If you look at a woman with lust, you have already committed adultery. Control your eyes (5:27).

6. When you pray, pray by yourself and in secret and you will be rewarded (6:6).

7. Don't repeat the same prayers over and over (6:7).

8. God knows what you need before you even ask him (6:8).

9. A recommended prayer listed in Matthew 6; verses 9-13, goes like this:

   "Our Father in heaven, we honor your holy name. We ask that your kingdom will come now. May your will be done here on earth, just as it is in heaven. Give us our food again today as usual, and forgive us our sins, just as we have forgiven those who have sinned against us. Don't bring us into temptation, but deliver us from the Evil One. Amen."

10. If someone sins against you, forgive them, and God will forgive you (6:14-15).

11. You are in spiritual darkness if your eyesight is blurred with evil thoughts and desires (6:22).

12. It is impossible to serve both God and money. You can only serve one master (6:24).

13. Since you already have life and a body, don't worry about what to eat and wear (6:25).

14. Don't worry because worrying does not have any benefits for your life (6:27).

15. Never worry about getting enough food and clothing, God will provide (6:31).

16. Obey God and put him first in your life and he will provide for all your needs (6:33).

17. Don't be overwhelmed with life's struggles; live life one day at a time (6:34).

18. Don't criticize others. If you do, you will be criticized (7:1).

19. If you need something, ask God to provide it for you and if it is in his will for you, it will be provided (7:7).

20. Do to others as you would want them to do to you (7:12).

21. Only a few find their way to the narrow gate of heaven (7:13).

22. If you publicly deny God to others, God will deny you (10:33).

23. God did not come to bring peace on earth, but rather a sword. If you love your parents more than God, you are not worthy of being of God (10:34, 37).

24. To be worthy, God wants you to take up the cross and follow him (10:38).

25. If you open your arms to good and godly men, you will reap rewards similar to theirs (10:41).

26. If you are a Christian, a representative of God and you give a child a cup of water, you will be rewarded by God (10:42).

27. Those who don't doubt God are blessed (11:6).

28. There is only one unforgiving sin and that is to speak against the Holy Spirit (12:31-32).

29. You will be held accountable for every idle word you speak, so watch your tongue (12:36).

30. God will have his angels separate out every temptation, and all who are evil will be thrown into the furnace of fire (13:41).

31. The faith of a small mustard seed can move mountains; nothing is impossible (17:20).

32. Don't cause anyone to lose their faith in God (18:6).

33. If two or more are gathered, God is there to provide anything they ask for (18:19).

34. Being perfect means to sell everything you have and give the money to the poor (19:21).

35. It is very difficult for a rich man to make it into heaven (19:23).

36. If you truly believe, you can get anything only by asking in prayer (21:22).

37. The most important command is to love the Lord with all your heart, soul and mind. The second most important command is to love your neighbor (22:37-39).

38. Being a servant is associated with greatness (23:11).

39. If you are not prepared for God's coming and you continue to have evil ways, sin and use drugs, God will come unannounced and will punish you severely (24:48).

40. Since no one knows of God's return he wants us to stay alert and be prepared for his coming (25:13).

41. If you refuse to help fellow Christians, it is the same as refusing to help God (25:45).

In Matthew, God tells us that obedience to every word of his is what we need. We need to be humble and not boast or be so proud. Don't partake in the evilness of sexual lust. Lusting is just as bad as committing the act itself. God will hold you accountable for your anger, cursing of others, disrespecting others, etc. Pray by yourself and in secret. God knows what you are going to ask him before it is asked. Don't recite the same prayer. Be a servant of only him and not with the things of the flesh and this world. Don't deny God to others or be ashamed you belong to God. Forgive others so God can forgive you. Don't worry about where your next meal will come from. Live one day at a time and don't worry about things. The only unforgiving sin is that against the Holy Spirit. Having just a little faith can move mountains. If you need anything, just ask for it in prayer. Having two or more people in prayer guarantees God's presence. The most important command is to love God with all your heart, soul, and mind. The second is to love your neighbor. Be prepared for the Lord's coming and turn from your evil ways. It is difficult for a rich man to get into to heaven! God wants us to love him even more than our mother or father, son or daughter. One may believe God wants to bring peace to the earth, but he really wants to bring a sword to separate good and evil.

The book of Matthew is the first book in the New Testament, where it begins to tell of the birth of Jesus. The book contains a lot of words of wisdom for us to go by in our daily lives.

MARK

1. You may harm your soul by what you think and say (7:15-16).

2. What makes man unfit for God is evil thoughts of lust, theft, murder, adultery, pride, slander, lewdness, deceit, and other wickedness (7:20-23).

3. To really live is to throw away your life for God's sake (8:35).

4. If you are ashamed of God, he too will be ashamed of you upon his return with the holy angels (8:38).

5. You will be rewarded if you provide a simple cup of water to someone just because they are a Christian (9:41).

6. Having faith in God is considered to be the absolute truth. All God wants you to do is

believe and have no doubt. Last but not least, listen to what he is trying to tell you (11:22-23).

7. Forgive those you have a grudge against so God will forgive you for your sins (11:25).

8. You will be hated because you belong to God. Those who endure to the end will be saved (13:13).

In Mark, God conveys to us that our souls may be harmed by what we think and say. Having evil and sinful thoughts will make us unfit for God and his blessings. God will reward those who do kind things. Having faith is the absolute truth. Have no doubt. You can pray for anything, and if you believe, you will have it. Forgive your enemies so God can forgive you. God again is asking for your trust and obedience. He is teaching us to "Do right."

LUKE

1. God wants you to do good deeds for your enemies. Pray for your enemies (6:27-28).

2. Ask for God's blessing for your enemies (6:28).

3. If someone asks for something that belongs to you, give it to them and don't worry about getting it back (6:30).

4. Love your enemies and show goodness in your heart to them (6:35).

5. If your enemy wants a loan, give it to him and don't be concerned if it will be repaid (6:35).

6. Don't condemn your neighbor (6:36).

7. God wants you to treat others like he would treat them. If you do, you will be greatly rewarded (6:31).

8. If you are good, you will do good deeds, and it will be deep down in your heart (6:45).

9. One will communicate what is actually in his heart (6:45).

10. Don't call upon the Lord unless you are willing to obey him (6:46).

11. When you listen to God, make sure you obey him (6:49).

12. Don't lose faith in God, and you will be blessed (7:23).

13. Anyone who loses his life for God will save his. Anyone that clings to their worldly life will lose it (9:24).

14. Those are considered great who care for others (9:48).

15. One is unfit for heaven if they lose track of God's plan for their lives (9:62).

16. God says that for you to live forever in heaven, you must love the Lord with all your heart, soul, strength, and mind, and secondly, love your neighbor (10:27).

17. Knock on the door, and God will answer. All those who seek will find. All those who ask will receive (11:9).

18. If you are not for God, you are against him. Publicly acknowledge God to others (11:23).

19. How generous you are demonstrates your purity (11:41).

20. Bless God for what you have; don't worry what you don't have (12:22).

21. Make God your primary concern in this world. Listen and obey. He knows what you need (12:30).

22. If you know your duty and refuse to do it, you will be punished (12:47).

23. If you don't know what you are doing is wrong, you will still receive some sort of punishment (12:48).

24. God does not come to provide peace and joy but rather strife and division (12:51).

25. Seek what is right and pursue it (12:57).

26. If you don't know God, does God know you? (13:23).

27. Some men that are despised on earth will be honored in heaven. Some that are prominent

in our world will be least important in heaven (13:30).

28. Those will be honored that are the most humbled (14:11).

29. Be honest in big and small matters (16:10).

30. God knows your most inner thoughts (16:15).

31. You will always be tempted to sin (17:1).

32. No matter how many times your brother sins against you, you are to forgive him (17:4).

33. You don't deserve praise just for obeying God. You are doing just what you are supposed to be doing (17:10).

34. When God returns, the day-to-day activities will be normal as usual (17:30).

In Luke, God wants us to love our enemies and pray for them. He wants us to do good deeds. Be generous and give to those who don't have. If someone wants something from you, you are to give it to them and not expect it to be returned. Don't criticize or condemn others. If you give, you will get. You can tell a man is good by what he says, because it comes from the heart. The measure of greatness is how you care for others. Don't deny God; obey him and you will receive his blessings. Be watchful and always be prepared for his coming. God's purpose for us is to separate us from good and evil. The evil will be destroyed. Get on the good side and have everlasting life. You will always have the temptation to sin. God is teaching us in Luke how to be a good Christian by helping others.

JOHN

1. You have to be born again to get into heaven (3:3).

2. The Holy Spirit provides the new life to us (3:6).

3. You must believe in God to have eternal life. God sacrificed his son on the cross so that our sins may be forgiven and that we have the opportunity to have eternal life with God (3:15-16).

4. Those who don't believe and obey him will never see heaven (3:36).

5. God leaves all judgment of sin to his son, Jesus, so that all will honor him. Jesus passes no judgment without talking with God (5:22).

6. No one can come to Jesus unless God attracts them to him (6:65). The Holy Spirit is the one that provides eternal life (6:63).

7. Follow and obey God so you won't stumble in life (8:12).

8. God said if we live as he tells us to, we will know the truth, and the truth will set us free (8:31).

9. Don't love your life on earth; exchange it for eternal life (12:25).

10. God will reveal himself to those who really love him and obey him (14:23).

11. Having peace of mind and heart is a gift. The Holy Spirit will teach us much if we listen (14:26-27).

12. Love each other as much as God loves us (15:12).

13. You don't choose God; he chooses you! (15:16).

14. Those who don't know God will criticize those who love and obey God (15:21).

15. The sin of the world shows the disbelief in God (16:9).

16. You will receive by using the name of Jesus (16:24).

In John, God tells us that we have to be born again to receive everlasting life in heaven. We must put our past behind us, including our sins, and begin listening to and obeying God. Do what God wants us to do. Do right. The Holy Spirit gives new life from heaven. Those who don't believe will not make it to heaven. God gives all judgment to Jesus, but Jesus passes no judgment without consulting with God. We are attracted to Jesus because of God's will. Don't cling to this world, but aspire to get to heaven. God will only reveal himself to those who love and obey him. Having peace is a gift from God. People will persecute Christians because they belong to God and they don't know him. This is evident by the sins of the world. Ask using Jesus's name, and it will be given. Have you been chosen and drawn to God? Many of God's un-chosen people are in prisons and jails today. Many of those in prisons and jails are of Satan and not of God. However, there are some of God's children also in prison and jails. Some of God's closest followers ended up in prison, such as John the Baptist and Peter and Paul, as seen in the book of Acts. Therefore, there is hope. When will it be time to make another path for yourself?

ACTS

1. Anyone asking God for mercy will receive it and will also receive salvation (2:21).

2. You will receive the Holy Spirit, which is a gift from God. You will then turn from your sin and be baptized for the forgiveness of your sins (2:38).

3. God released Peter from prison by using angels to come get him out of his cell. His restraints fell off of him, and doors and gates came open, allowing him to walk out. Nothing is impossible, and one must have hope. All you have to do is love and obey God and do what he wants you to do (12:6-19).

4. To trust God is to be free from guilt (13:39).

5. God gave us another example when a mob formed against Paul and Silas. Paul and Silas were later thrown into prison. Paul and Silas

began praying and singing to God. Suddenly there was a great earthquake, and the prison was shaken off its foundation. All the doors flew open, and the chains of every inmate fell off. The jailer, believing all inmates had escaped, drew his sword to commit suicide, but before killing himself, he asked what he must do to be saved. They told him, and he was saved (16:22-40).

In Acts, God says one must turn from sin, receive the Holy Spirit, and be baptized to show faith and begin the new journey, loving and obeying God. Examples from God's people were seen by God coming to the rescue of his followers by releasing them from prison. Don't give up hope; you can escape your situation.

ROMANS

1. Believers are sent around the world to tell people what God has done for them, so the others will believe and obey (1:5).

2. God will prepare us for heaven (1:17).

3. The only true way to find life is to find it through trusting God (1:17).

4. God gets angry with the evils of the world and from those who will not listen and obey (1:18).

5. Chosen people know God instinctively; he has put the knowledge in their hearts (1:19).

6. God is a very patient God. He will use restraint in punishing you if you disobey and don't listen to him (2:4).

7. His kindness will lead you to repent from your sins (2:4).

8. If you continue to disobey and sin in this world, God will punish you. The day will come when God's anger will be seen (2:5).

9. Wherever sin is found is where punishment will be evident (2:8).

10. People know right from wrong. People's own consciences know sin and evilness (2:12-15).

11. God will one day unveil one's innermost thoughts and intentions (2:16).

12. We have all sinned and have fallen short of God's expectations (3:23).

13. God sent his son, Jesus, to the world to take the punishment for our sins. This ended God's anger toward the sinful people (3:25).

14. We are not exonerated solely on our good deeds (3:27).

15. People are saved by our faith in God, not by the good things we do in this world (3:28).

16. Being saved is a gift from God (4:4).

17. When we run into problems, we can ask God for his intervention and to show us the way. It

helps us to be obedient and dependent on God (5:3).

18. Patience gives us strength and helps us find hope and faith in God. The Holy Spirit fills our heart, and we can feel God's glory and grace (5:4).

19. The power of sin is broken when we get saved and baptized. We put our sinful nature behind us. Jesus died on the cross so our sins can be forgiven by God (6:2-3).

20. When we die, we can rise like Jesus rose from his death (6:5).

21. Our evil desires were nailed to the cross with Jesus (6:6).

22. Do not let sin control our bodies, and do not give into sin and evil ways. Be strong (6:11).

23. Don't let any part of your body be used for sinful things and wickedness. You want your body to be used by God to do the things he wants you to do (6:12-13).

24. Sin shall never be your master again. You are free from sin (6:18).

25. Be obedient to God and bury your sins (6:18).

26. The wages of sin is death (6:23).

27. Only those who have the Spirit in Christ living in them are true Christians (8:9).

28. Pray that the Holy Spirit crushes your evil deeds and thoughts. You are strong enough to turn away from the temptations of sin. You have no obligation to return to your old, sinful ways (8:12).

29. Pray every day and ask God to give you the strength and obedience to do right and turn from evilness and sin (8:26).

30. The Holy Spirit prays for us when we pray to God. He conveys the message with expressed feelings and words much better than we can do (8:26).

31. God knows what the Spirit is saying, as it is in God's will for our lives (8:27).

32. God is kind to some people, and he makes some refuse to listen to him (9:18).

33. We can be saved by telling others that Jesus is our Lord and we believe that Jesus has been

raised from the dead and died on the cross for our sins (10.9).

34. No one will be disappointed if they believe in God (10:11).

35. Anyone that calls out to God will be saved (10:13).

36. God is hard on those who disobey and good to those who love and obey him. If you continue to disobey, you will be cut off (11:22).

37. Since God's spirit lives within you, he wants your bodies to be a living sacrifice to him (12:1).

38. Don't pretend you love your neighbor; really love them (12:9).

39. Hate what is wrong and pursue what is right. Stand on the good side and be glad for God's plan in your life (12:9).

40. Protect and stand up for what is good and right (12:9).

41. In troubled times, be patient and pray often (12:12).

42. If someone mistreats you because you are a Christian, ask God through prayer to bless them (12:14).

43. If others are joyful, be joyful with them (12:15).

44. If others are mourning, mourn with them (12:15).

45. Don't try to hang around and get in the good graces of important and powerful people. Enjoy the common folk (12:16).

46. Never fight evil with evil but with loving kindness (12:17).

47. Be transparent in all you do so people see that you are good and honest (12:17).

48. Don't fight with anyone, for it is not worth it (12:18).

49. Seek and be at peace with all things (12:18).

50. Don't try to enforce the laws; let those with the authority do so (12:19).

51. Feed your enemy, and he will be shameful and regret the misgivings he has caused you (12:20).

52. Conquer evil by doing good (12:21).

53. Obey and respect the government. A government exists only because God allows it (13:1).

54. Those who disobey the laws of the world are refusing to obey God (13:2).

55. Obey the laws to keep from punishment, but do it because it is the right thing to do. This is what God wants you to do (13:5).

56. God wants us to pay our taxes so the government workers can continue to do God's work, serving the people (13:6).

57. Ensure you pay your debts (13:8).

58. God wants you to love your neighbors as you love yourself (13:9).

59. It is good to be living right, since we may be approaching the coming of the Lord (13:11).

60. God wants you to put on the armor of right living and give up the evil deeds you continue to do (13:12-13).

61. Don't make plans to enjoy evil, but spend your valuable time doing God's work (13:12-13).

62. Don't criticize those who don't share your same ideals (14:2).

63. Each one of us will have to give an account of ourselves to God. Never make your brother stumble by letting him see you doing something he believes to be wrong (14:12-13).

64. Avoid being in a position to be criticized, even though what you are doing is right (14:16).

65. Don't do anything that offends another, even if you are doing right (14:21).

66. Anything you do that you feel is not right is a sin (14:23).

67. Be clear in what is right and what is wrong. Know your boundaries (16:19).

In Romans, God says he prepares us for heaven. We must trust and obey God. God has chosen us. God will punish us for our sins and wrong doing. We have all fallen short of God's expectations. We are saved by our faith in God, not by our good works on earth. We are saved by turning against our sinful nature as we begin a new journey obeying and trusting God. Our bodies should not be used in a sinful manner but kept whole to do God's work. The Holy Spirit takes our prayers and translates them into a much-pronounced manner, as only the Holy Spirit can do. We are not to be proud, but humble, grateful, and careful. Stand on the side of good and righteousness. Be glad for all God is planning. Don't quarrel with others and don't do things that offend others. Obey the laws on earth, because it is the right thing to do. Pay taxes, so workers can continue to do God's work for the people. Pay your debts. Be prepared for God's coming and stay right.

Many believe that choosing to work in prisons and jails is actually a calling from God; that is where God wanted them to be. In Romans, it tells us how one is to be saved. You must believe that God's son, Jesus, died on the cross so that our sins can be forgiven and we may have eternal life with God. Jesus died on the cross and was raised on the third day and went to heaven to be with his Father. We commit to putting our sinful and evil ways behind us, and we start a new journey, believing, obeying, and trusting God for all we do, think, and say. Being baptized is a public profession of washing away our old nature and being born a new person, committed to doing God's will.

1 CORINTHIANS

1. Only the chosen ones from God can understand the thoughts from God and what the Holy Spirit teaches us (2:14).

2. We are not to associate with one that participates in sexual sins, is greedy, worships idols, is abusive, or is a drunkard. We are to stay clear of these types of people (5:11).

3. We are to run from sexual sin. When we sin against our own body, we are hurting the Holy Spirit, who lives within us (6:18).

4. If you stay single, that is good. It may be best for many to marry to help one from sinning (7:1-2).

5. A husband must never divorce his wife, and a wife should not leave her husband (7:10-11).

6. If a Christian's wife is not a Christian herself but chooses to stay, the husband should not leave her or divorce her (7:12).

7. If either one of them is not a Christian and wants to leave, they may (7:15).

8. When one is saved, he should continue what he is doing (7:20).

9. No temptation is irresistible. God can provide you the tools to avoid falling into sin. You have to be strong and trust God (10:13).

10. God can and will show you how to avoid the temptation of sin (10:13).

11. When God punishes us, we suffer so we are not condemned with others of the world (11:32).

12. Our greatest focus should be on loving others (14:1).

13. Remember to tithe ten percent of what you receive (16:2).

In 1 Corinthians, God reminds us not to keep company that has a negative impact upon us. We are not to associate with sinners. We are to run from sexual sin and avoid temptation and using our bodies to sin. The Holy Spirit is within us, and using our bodies to sin is hurting the Holy Spirit. It is good to be single in life, but it may help others from sinning if they do marry. We should not divorce or leave our spouses. If one is not a Christian and wants to leave, it is permissible. When you are saved, God wants you to keep doing what you were doing. He wants us to consistently tithe our first ten percent to ensure we keep God first in our lives. Applying these principals will enhance our Christian life. It is very easy; don't sin, stay focused, obey and trust God for all your needs and wisdom.

2 CORINTHIANS

1. God will comfort us in our troubles and hardships. He will give us the strength to endure (1:3-4,7).

2. Our troubles are only temporary, but God's blessing is forever (4:17).

3. God is ready to save us (6:2).

4. We should patiently go through our troubles, knowing God is always there for us (6:4).

5. Don't partner up with those who do not love the Lord (6:14).

6. If you give little, expect little (9:6).

7. It is good to have less because it causes you to depend on the Lord even more (12:10).

In 2 Corinthians, the Lord reminds us that he is there to provide comfort in our difficult times. He will provide strength and direction for us. Our troubles are only temporary. We must stay strong and patient and ride out the storms in our lives. You have to maintain hope and patience and be obedient and trusting in God. Live day by day. It won't be easy to be a Christian, and you will have trials, struggles, and obstacles. You have to stay focused and keep moving forward. Try to be a better Christian today than what you were yesterday.

GALATIANS

1. We find life by trusting and having faith in God (3:11).

2. We are to love others (5:14).

3. Stay focused on the instructions of the Holy Spirit. We naturally love to sin and engage in evil deeds. This is totally opposite of what we should be doing (5:16).

4. We cannot rely on ourselves but must draw strength from God to help us from sinning and committing evil deeds (5:19).

5. When we turn our lives over to God, he will bring us love, joy, peace, patience, kindness, goodness, faithfulness, gentleness, and self-control (5:22).

6. You cannot run away from God; he will eventually catch up with you. You will get the punishment you deserve in the end (6:7).

In Galatians, God conveys to us that he wants us to love others and have faith in him. He wants us to obey the instructions of the Holy Spirit. We, by nature, love to sin. When we allow God to control our lives, all the pieces fall in place and we find the true things God wants us to experience, for example, peace and joy. God will hold us accountable for our sins. You will be punished for your sins. He is shaping us to be godly. We are not perfect, and temptation will always be there. We just have to continue to make the right decision and trust that God will give us the strength, endurance, and wisdom to get through it.

EPHESIANS

1. God wants us to be humble and gentle, because he chose us and he gives us the Holy Spirit to strengthen us (4:2-3).

2. We are to be patient with one another. God has given us all special abilities (4:3,7).

3. God does not want us to go to bed still angry with anyone (4:26).

4. If one is stealing, he must stop immediately and begin using his hands for God's work (4:28).

5. Don't cause the Holy Spirit to mourn because of your lifestyle and continued sinning (4:30).

6. Quit being mean to others, having a temper and screaming and yelling. Why do you quarrel and curse at others? These things should not be a part of your life or lifestyle. Be full of love and not hate (4:31-32).

7. Eradicate any sexual sin, impurity, or greed you have in you (5:3).

8. Don't put greed in front of God (5:5).

9. Always remember to do what is right and true (5:9).

10. Expose and turn against evilness in the world (5:11).

11. Take every opportunity to do good (5:15-16).

12. Don't drink too much, because you will cross many evils that way (5:18).

13. Children are directed to obey their parents and honor their mothers and fathers (6:1-2).

14. God says he will pay you for each good deed you do (6:8).

15. Your strength must come from the Lord's mighty power within you. Put on all of God's armor so that you will be able to stand safe against all strategies and tricks of Satan. Use every piece of God's armor to resist the enemy whenever he attacks, and when it is all over, you will still be standing up (6:10-13).

16. Resist the enemy whenever he attacks; stand strong and put your trust and faith in God, and he will not let you down (6:13).

17. God wants us to pray to him all the time. Pray for other Christians in the world (6:18).

In Ephesians, Gods tells us to be humble and gentle. Be patient with one another, and we all have special abilities given to us by God. Don't stay angry with others; love one another. Always do right. Take every chance to be good and do good deeds. The Lord will reward us for each good deed we do in life. God wants to hear our prayers and wants us to pray for all Christians. Don't be under the influence of intoxicating beverages or substances because of what it brings with it—evilness.

PHILIPPIANS

1. God doesn't want us to be selfish, always trying to impress others. He wants us to be humble (2:3).

2. God does not want us to complain and argue among one another (2:14).

3. Whatever troubles we have and obstacles we face, always be glad in the Lord (3:1).

4. Don't fret over little things, but pray about everything (4:6).

5. Always let God know what your needs are and then thank him. By doing this, you will find God's peace (4:6).

6. Focus on what is good, true, and righteous (4:8).

In Philippians, Paul is writing to fellow Christians while he is in prison. He believed God put him there to defend the truth about God. Paul was there gladly, and he knew it would all turn out good in the end. God tells us not to be selfish and try to impress others. He wants us to be humble and to think of others. He wants us to live in harmony and to not complain, argue, and fight. He wants us to live a clean and innocent life. He wants us to be glad in the Lord. He wants us to pray and convey what our needs are to him. He wants us to have peace. Get in the practice and customs of doing right!

COLOSSIANS

1. God will free you from evil desires if you seek him (2:11).

2. God tells us not to worry and not to seek the desires of this world. Our real life is in heaven (3:2-3).

3. It is not productive to have strong desires for this world. We should focus on the next life in heaven (3:5).

4. Husbands should be loving and kind to their wives (3:19).

5. God tells fathers not to discourage their children by scolding them too often. They will eventually quit trying (3:21).

6. God wants us to work hard and be cheerful while doing it. We are really doing God's work here on earth (3:23-24).

In Colossians, God says he will set us free from our evil desires if we seek him. He tells us not to worry and that the real life is in heaven with him. He wants husbands to be loving and kind to their wives and not be bitter or harsh toward them. He doesn't want fathers to be strict on children so that they become discouraged and quit trying to please their fathers. Don't belittle your children; encourage them. God wants us to work hard and to be glad doing it. We should not love this world or worldly things but look forward to our everlasting life.

2 THESSALONIANS

1. God uses your suffering to make you ready for heaven. He will also punish those who hurt you (1:4-6).

2. God tells those who are suffering that he will give them rest when he returns. Those not of God will be punished in hell (1:7-9).

3. You will one day belong to him, and that will be your greatest glory (1:12).

4. God wants us never to stop doing what is right (3:13).

In 2 Thessalonians, God reassures those who are suffering in this world that he will restore their rest upon his return. God wants us to continue to do right. Suffering is sometimes not a bad thing, and it is used to mold us and get us ready for heaven. He will hold his children accountable for their actions, thoughts, desires, and evilness.

1 TIMOTHY

1. God wants us to exercise spiritually and practice being a better Christian for this world and the world to be (4:8).

2. Be focused on all you do and think (4:16).

3. Do what is right, and God will bless you (4:16).

4. Be respectful to older people (5:1).

5. The love of money is the first step toward a multitude of sins (6:10).

6. The rich are not to be proud and place all their faith on their money (6:17).

7. The rich people should use their money to do good deeds and good works and share with others what God has given them. God will reward them in heaven (6:17-19).

In 1 Timothy, we are told to exercise ourselves spiritually and prepare ourselves to do better for this world and the next. We need to be careful and watch everything we say and do. We are to stay true to God's word and always respect the elderly. The rich are not to be proud, but use their money to do God's work and share their wealth and they will be blessed.

2 TIMOTHY

1. God will provide strength in times of suffering. If we turn against God, he will turn against us (1:8).

2. Always strive to make God proud of us, and he will say one day, "Well done" (2:15).

3. Don't get engaged in foolish discussions. It only leads to anger (2:16).

4. A person who calls himself a Christian should not be doing things that are wrong (2:19).

5. Run from sin and evilness. Stay close to doing right (2:22).

6. It is going to be hard to remain a Christian in the last days, so be aware (3:1).

7. It is okay to be afraid of suffering for the Lord as you bring others to him (4:5).

8. God can and will deliver us from all wickedness and evilness (4:18).

9. God gave us the Bible to inspire us and keep us on the right track. It is a tool to keep us on the straight and narrow (3:16-17).

In 2 Timothy, God says he will comfort and strengthen us during times of suffering. We must never turn against God but remain obedient and faithful. We should strive to make God proud of us. We should work hard in doing good and run away from evil and sin. Things will get tough, but we must pull together and keep our faith and trust in God. God will always deliver us from evil. The Bible was provided to us to keep us on the right track of knowing the truth and keeping the faith. Being in a prison or jail cell may not be the best environment to practice Christianity, so those folks may have to work a little harder, pray more, stay focused, and be in the Word on a regular basis. There is hope.

TITUS

1. A good person always finds the good in everything. An evil person finds evil in everything (1:15).

2. God strives for all of us to live a good, God-fearing life each and every day (2:11).

3. God rescued us from continuous sinning and renewed our souls so we can do good deeds (2:14).

4. Don't get into a debate; it really has little or no value (3:9).

In Titus, God tells us that a good man sees good in everything. God wants us to live a true and good life each day. Jesus died so we can live and have another life without sin and evil. He doesn't want us to get into arguments, debates, and unanswerable questions and controversial ideas. It only does harm and has little value. He wants us to have a good disposition and attitude.

HEBREWS

1. Angels carry spirit messages out to God's chosen ones (1:14).

2. God has given each believer special gifts from the Holy Spirit (2:4).

3. Jesus died for us, and since he lived in this world, he is fully aware what it is like to suffer and receive temptations (2:18).

4. Always listen to God and don't ignore him (3:15).

5. We can never hide anything from God. He knows all (4:12-13).

6. If you sin purposely and reject God after knowing the truth of forgiveness, the sin is not covered by the death of Jesus and there is no way to get rid of it (10:26).

7. We need to be consistent in doing God's work and being obedient (10:35).

8. Having faith secures your salvation (10:39).

9. God rewards those who seek him out (11:6).

10. Don't get mad at God for punishing you for your sins. He is teaching you the right way, so don't be discouraged. Keep your eyes on him and stay focused (12:5-7).

11. We should support one another and ensure we do not sin or fail (12:15).

12. We should fear God and serve him with thankful hearts (12:28).

13. We should be kind to strangers (13:2).

14. We should suffer with those who are incarcerated; we should never forget those behind bars. We should show them the way (13:3).

15. Share in other's sorrows, as we all experience it one time or another (13:3).

16. Be content with what you have. Don't fall in love with money (13:5).

17. God will never fail or forsake you. You are not alone; he is there with you at all times (13:5).

18. Spiritual strength is a gift from God, and it will assist you in becoming a better Christian (13:9).

In Hebrews, God tells us that angels are spirit messengers sent out to care for God's people. Each believer has special gifts provided by God. Jesus knows what it's like to be tempted and what it is like to suffer also. We should listen to God and not ignore what he tries to tell us. We cannot hide from God; he is everywhere and knows everything. We need to take care of one another and show support. This will help us from sinning. We need to be patient and continue to seek his will for our lives. We should see punishment as an opportunity to learn rather than to be discouraged. God wants us to be kind to strangers and not forget those who are in our prisons and jails. We should share our sorrows with those who are mistreated, as many of us can relate to similar experiences. Prison ministry is a good example of how people care for those in our prisons and jails. It is a true calling of God. The prison volunteers are special people, dedicated and loyal to their mission. They are a gift from God who carry God's message to those who cling to hope and those willing to listen and turn from their sin.

JAMES

1. When times get rough, your patience has the opportunity to grow and flourish (1:3).

2. If you ever wonder what God wants you to do, all you have to do is ask him and he will reveal his will to you (1:5).

3. A person shouldn't have to worry about if they amount to much in this world, based on worldly standards. It really doesn't matter, because the Lord sees a Christian to be great (1:9).

4. God will reward us with the crown of life if we avoid temptation and stay strong (1:12).

5. Temptation is the flesh's attraction to our own evil thoughts and desires (1:14).

6. We will end in death if we pursue our evil thoughts, which eventually lead to evil acts (1:15).

7. It is better to listen than to talk too much (1:19).

8. We should work hard to not become angry, because anger is not a good thing (1:20).

9. Seek to get rid of all the wrongs in your life and be humbly gracious to do so (1:21).

10. A pure Christian is one who takes care of orphans and widows (1:27).

11. One that makes a little mistake is just as guilty as one that has broken many laws (2:10).

12. God will judge you by what you are doing in this world compared to what God wants you to do (2:12).

13. Be careful what you think and say, for God will have no mercy for those who have no mercy for others (2:12).

14. Display your faith through your good works. If you don't have good works, it is hard to prove your devoted faith. So, go out and do good works for God to see (2:17).

15. You can display faith by your actions: what you say, what you do, what you believe in (2:18).

16. Without completing what God wants you to do, believing is useless (2:19).

17. Don't be quick to point out blemishes in others, for do we not have any blemishes ourselves? (3:1).

18. Restraining your tongue is having control and self-discipline in your life (3:1-2).

19. Although the tongue is a small part of your body, it can cause great hurt, distress, and damage to others (3:5).

20. A tongue is said to be similar to a flame of fire. It is full of wickedness (3:6).

21. Don't boast about being so wise and good if you have sin in your life (3:14).

22. Some don't have what they want because they have not asked God for it. Ask God for what you need and want and leave the rest up to him. Be patient (4:2).

23. God will provide your needs and wants if it is within his will. If you don't get what you want, there is a reason for it (4:3).

24. Be careful and do not associate with the enemy of God, which are the sinful pleasures of the flesh. If you do, it makes you an enemy of God (4:4).

25. Be strong and resist Satan, and he will leave you and go elsewhere (4:7).

26. Stay near God, and he will stay near you (4:7).

27. When you become humble and admit your sin and that you have fallen short of the glory of God, God will pick you up and provide comfort and encouragement to you (4:9-10).

28. Do not criticize others and gossip among one another. Be careful what comes out of your mouth. Control your tongue. Be self-disciplined (4:11).

29. If you do not do what you know is right, it is a sin (4:17).

30. If you are suffering, pray (5:13).

31. Let God know if you are thankful for what he has done or will do in your life (5:13).

James tells us that if we want to know what God wants us to do, all we have to do is ask him, and he will show us. Even though we may not be much in this world, we are great in God's eyes. We will be rewarded with the crown of life if we will only turn our backs to sin and not give in to temptation. Evil thoughts result in evil acts, so be careful and control your thoughts. Stop it right then; don't let the sinful thoughts enter your mind. It is always better to be quiet and speak little. We can control what we say much easier if we stop and think before we say anything. Make sure it is good and righteous and not critical or hurtful. Seek to get rid of all that is wrong in our lives and be glad about it, as well as humble. We will be held accountable for even our simple mistakes; we are just as guilty as those who sin frequently. God wants us to prove our faith by our good works. We are also judged by what we do and say. Ask God to provide for your needs and wants, and if it is God's will and it is in accordance with his plan for you, it will be granted. Be patient. Be close to God, and he will be close to you. Thank God for your blessing and the gifts he has provided to you. Trust him.

1 PETER

1. God chose you a long time ago, and he knew if you would be a child of God or not (1:2).

2. The Holy Spirit works in your heart when you may not even know it or realize it. It soon will show itself in your life. Be aware of the power of the Holy Spirit (1:2).

3. Joy, peace, and comfort are just around the corner; seek and find them (1:7).

4. God may test your faith to see if you are strong and pure or weak and deceitful (1:7).

5. God will reward those who have a strong foundation of faith and have passed the test. He will honor you one day (1:7).

6. Stay focused on being good and pure. Don't let others drag you down to your old ways (1:14).

7. Don't hate; love your neighbor. This is God's wish (2:1).

8. Don't talk the talk without walking the walk. Don't just talk the good deeds; go out and do them (2:1).

9. Quit the gossiping. It is hurtful, and God despises it (2:1).

10. We are only on earth for a short time. It is temporary. We are considered to be only visitors during our time on earth (2:11).

11. Be aware of how you act with your saved and unsaved neighbors (2:12).

12. Be kind, gentle, and respectful to all and yourself (2:17).

13. You will experience suffering in this world, just like everyone else. How will you deal with it? (2:21).

14. Don't get consumed with how you look or the jewelry you have or the clothes on your back. Focus on God's will in your life and doing what God wants you to do. Don't be consumed by others, but be consumed by God (3:3).

15. We are to pursue having a kind and gentle heart and doing what is right in God's eyes. Perfect is doing what is right (3:4).

16. Don't act negatively because others treat you badly. Do what is right. Don't copy sin for sin (3:9).

17. When someone criticizes you, don't react with hurtful words for them (3:9).

18. One can have a good and successful life if they control their tongue and prevent telling lies (3:10).

19. Flee from evil and focus on doing good and what is right (3:11).

20. God will hold those who are evil accountable for their actions (3:12).

21 God wants us to just do the right thing! Practice it and don't work so hard in doing evil, sinful things. Use this time to perfect goodness (3:16).

22. If you must suffer, suffer by going out and doing good works. It's much better than suffering while doing wrong (3:17).

23. When we are baptized, we are asking God to cleanse our hearts from sin and begin a new life with a new direction (3:21).

24. When one suffers, sin loses its power, so be ready to suffer. It is not a bad thing (4:1).

25. Show love for one another. It is healthy because it overshadows our sins (4:8).

26. When you are mocked because you are a Christian, delight in it. God will honor those who are strong and steadfast. It is not shameful to be a Christian (4:14,16).

27. Trust God in everything you do. He will never fail you (4:19).

28. When things get to tough for you, let go and let God take control of your worries. Turn it over to God and leave the rest to him. He will help you if you will listen and obey him (5:7).

29. Be aware of Satan's presence and his desire to attack you and bring you down. Stay focused on God to pull you through any situation, big or small (5:8-9).

30. After God allows you to suffer awhile, he will pick you up and comfort you. You will be a better person for going through the experience (5:10).

In 1 Peter, God reveals many secrets to us. He tells us that he has chosen each of us to be a child of God years ago. The Holy Spirit has been inside of us, working on us and bringing us around to be prepared to listen and obey God. God will test us, and we will endure pain and suffering. Everything happens for a reason. God wants us to stay focused, trust and love him, obey him, and listen to him. He wants us to love others and not pay evil for evil or snap back at others for what they say to us. Don't worry about worldly things, but focus on your future with God and do what he wants you to do. Seek his will for your life. Be aware of what you say and how you act. Live in peace and be happy to be a Christian. You will receive your reward in heaven.

2 PETER

1. Strive to learn all you can about God and seek his will for you. Work hard to be good and do not resist God and what he wants for you. Accept what God wants for you and let him be in charge of your life (1:2-3).

2. Prove by your actions that you are a child of God and you have been chosen to be a child of God. Don't disappoint God and stumble along the way (1:10).

3. Every day, try hard to do good and not to sin. Take it day by day (3:14).

In 2 Peter, the message is clear. Strive to learn all you can about God and his will he has for you. He has a plan for you; seek it, find it, and do it. Work hard every day to be good and not sin. Put aside your own desires and live for God. Show others you are a child of God and you have been chosen. Don't let God down. Just don't sin. You have to trust him.

1 JOHN

1. If you claim to be a Christian, it is wise to live like one all the time (2:6).

2. As we love one another and do what is right, the new life will be clear to others (2:8).

3. Don't love this world and all it has to offer. It is full of sin and wickedness. Sexual sin, possessions, pride, wealth, and importance are not from God... Beware (2:15).

4. Those of us that continue to sin are against God. It is not God's will for us to sin (3:4).

5. If you continue to sin, you become a child of Satan and not a child of God. Is this what you want? (3:8).

6. We should strive to come to God with a clear conscience and not be bothered by our sins. How can we expect God to fulfill our needs and wishes when we continue to have sin in

our lives? Obey him and trust him, and you will feel comfortable in asking for his guidance (3:21).

7. We sometimes know when a message is from God because others won't listen to it (4:6).

8. Work hard and practice loving one another. This is God's will. This is what he wants us to do in this world. Love each other, support each other—do right (4:7).

9. You cannot be part of God's family if you continue to sin. If you are truly God's child, the devil will not be able to get his hands on you (5:18).

10. Don't get involved in things that will take the place of God in your lives. Devote everything to him (5:21).

First John says we should live as Christ did if we call ourselves Christians. As we practice being a Christian, we will develop a new life in Christ. Our old will become new. Don't love the things of this world, but keep your eyes on God to provide your needs. Focus on doing what God wants you to do.

Don't engage in the world's temptation and sins of sex, possessions, power, and authority. It is not from God. He has already told us that a rich man will have a hard time getting into heaven. Don't belong to Satan but belong to God. Not everyone will listen to God's message. Not all will be a child of God. Don't let anything interfere with your relationship to God whereas it takes the place of God in your life. Will you become a child of God or Satan?

3 JOHN

1. God wants us to take care of traveling teachers and those chosen to be missionaries. They are doing God's work, and we should help support them and provide them with encouragement and ensure that they continue their valuable work for the Lord (1:5).

Third John says we are to take care of those who teach others and those who are missionaries. Their work is good. Prison volunteers are also teachers; give them your respect.

JUDE

1. Know your parameters and beware not to cross that line that keeps you from God's blessings (1:21).

2. Have mercy for those who may doubt us or criticize us (1:22).

In Jude, we learn that God wants us to always be aware of our boundaries and that we do not get out of God's reach. He wants us near, and he wants us to beware when we have gone too far. Know your boundaries. Have mercy on those who may doubt us and our work, for they may not know. Be strong in your convictions and of the Word of God.

THE REVELATION

1. We are not to be afraid to suffer. Some of us may be placed in prison to test us. God wants us to remain faithful and put our trust in him (2:10).

2. Those who are victorious will not be harmed by the second death (2:11).

3. We will receive our due rewards in God's timing (2:26).

4. God is a merciful God. He knows our faults; he also knows our efforts and what is in our hearts. He knows if we have denied him. He will have mercy on those who deserve it (2:23).

5. The Great Tribulation will be a time God will test all. Those who have obeyed God will be protected and spared (3:10).

6. God will spit out those who are straddling the fence. You cannot be in the middle; you have

to be a child of God or not. You must obey and trust or not. It is your choice (3:15).

7. God tells us that he will discipline us and will punish us for our evil deeds. He does this to teach us and encourage us to stay on the right path. He does this because of his love for us (3:19).

8. We will all be judged by our deeds in the end. How have you acted? (20:13).

9. Those who have not had their name recorded in the Book of Life will perish and will be thrown in the lake of fire (20:15).

In Revelations, God tells us not to be afraid to suffer. He will allow Satan to throw some in prison as a test of our faith. Don't be discouraged and don't give up hope. Those should remain faithful, and if they are, they will receive the crown of life. God knows our strengths and weaknesses. He will have mercy on those who deserve it. God will spare those who have obeyed and trusted him and will protect them from the tribulation that is to come. God does not want us to be lukewarm. He does not want us to straddle the fence. He wants us to commit to him fully or not at all. Those who are not saved and have their name in the Book of Life will experience the lake of fire. What will you chose?

CONCLUSION

Now since we have read what God wants us to know and how we are to behave and interact with one another, let's review and highlight some of the words of wisdom God has for us.

God wants us to obey him and trust him. He wants us to put him first in all we do. God's most important command for us is to love the Lord with all our hearts, souls, and minds. The second most important command is to love our neighbors. He wants us to take care of the poor, widows, and orphans. He wants us to take care of teachers and missionaries. He wants us to have two goals: have wisdom and common sense. He does not want us to violate his commandments. He doesn't want us to murder, lie, steal, cheat, be jealous or envious of others and what others have, but to be content with what we have. He tells us to run from sexual sin. He doesn't want us to worry but, rather, have faith in him. He wants us to pray about everything and tell him what our needs are. He wants us to do good deeds and seek out what his will is in our lives and pursue it with all our hearts, minds, and souls. He does not want us to engage in sexual sin, drunkenness, or adultery or to love money or love this world more than we love him. He doesn't want us to argue, fight, and complain. He wants us to love him more than our fathers and mothers, brothers and sisters. He wants us to love and be kind to others. He wants us to have compassion. He wants us not to gossip and to control our tongues. He wants us to be humble and not proud or boastful. He doesn't want us to worship anything or anybody but him. He wants a personal relationship with us. He wants us to give the first of our earnings to him, to remind us to put him always first in our lives and he will bless us. He does not want us working on the Sabbath day. He wants us to forgive others who sin against us. He doesn't want us to sin, because he knows that will separate us from him. He wants us to know he has a plan for us.

God tells us he is in control of everything. We have all sinned and have fallen short of God's glorious ideal (Romans 3:23).

You can be content in prison and with your circumstances. The circumstances of incarceration may need to be painful so you can get it! Evil can be chased out of a man's heart if the punishment hurts enough (Proverbs 20:30). God tells us punishment is a good remedy for a rebellious fellow (Proverbs 22:15).

Focus on the positives rather than the negatives. "And we all know that all things that happen to us is working for our good if we love God and are fitting into his plans" (Romans 8:28). We need to focus on Jesus rather than our circumstances. Focus on God rather than man.

> Though I am surrounded by troubles, you
> will bring me safely through them. You will
> clench your fist against my angry enemies!
>
> Psalm 138:7

> O God, have pity, for I am trusting you! I
> will hide beneath the shadow of your wings
> until this storm is past. He will send down
> help from heaven to save me, because of his
> love and his faithfulness.
>
> Psalm 57: 1,3

Psalm 86 of the Living Bible states, in part:

> O God, bend down and hear my prayer and answer me, for I am deep in trouble. Protect me from death, for I try to follow all your laws. Save me, for I am serving you and trusting you. Be merciful, O Lord, for I am looking up to you in constant hope. O God, hear my urgent cry. I will call to you whenever trouble strikes and you will help me. Violent Godless men try to kill me. When those who hate me see it, they will lose face because you help and comfort me.

In Philippians 1:13, Paul writes while he is in prison:

> For everyone around here, including all the soldiers over at the barracks, knows that I am in chains simply because I am a Christian. And because of my imprisonment, many of the Christians here seem to have lost their fear of chains! Somehow my patience has encouraged them and they have become more and more bold in telling others about Christ."

Paul writes in a letter that he wants Christians to see clearly the difference between right and wrong and to be inwardly clean so no one will be able to criticize them. Paul states that everything that has happened to him in prison has been a great boost in getting out the Good News concerning Christ. He believed God brought him to prison so he could use him to defend the Truth. Paul committed to staying positive, because he knew the Holy Spirit was helping him and all things would turn out good in the end. Paul stated he would live in eager expectation and hope and that he would never do anything that would cause him to be ashamed of himself. He would always speak out boldly about Christ while he was in prison. He expected all Christians in prison to live a clean, innocent life as children of God in a dark world full of people who are angry, evil, and of Satan.

If you die today, are you ready? You can be saved by the grace of God by praying the following prayer:

> Oh God, I am a sinner and have fallen short of your glory. I realize my sins have caused me to be separated from you. I confess of my sins and ask for your forgiveness

and your loving kindness. I realize your
son Jesus died on the cross and rose on the
third day so that I may have eternal life. I
commit my life to you and agree to obey
your commandments and live by the words
of wisdom you have given us. Come into
my life and fill my heart, mind, and soul
with your glory and provide me the gift of
the Holy Spirit. In Jesus's name, amen.

It is also necessary to be baptized, which is a public
display to show you have been born again and you
are a new creature in Christ. Your sins have been
washed away.

But all these things that I once thought
very worthwhile—now I've thrown them
all away so that I can put my trust and hope
in Christ alone.

Philippians 3:7

But they that wait upon the Lord shall
renew their strength. They shall mount up
with wings like eagles; they shall run and
not be weary; they shall walk and not faint.

Isaiah 40:31

Fix your thoughts on what is true and good
and right!

Philippians 4:8

Do right!